Washington Avenue Branch
Albany Public Library

SEF

S0-AEO-079

One Vote, Two Votes, I Vote, You Vote

Voting is something
we do every day.
It's a way we can choose
that gives us our own say.

The Cat in the Hat's Learning Library® introduces beginning readers to basic non-fiction. If your child can read these lines, then he or she can begin to understand the fascinating world in which we live.

Learn to read. Read to learn.

This book comes from the home of

THE CAT IN THE HAT

RANDOM HOUSE

For a list of books in **The Cat in the Hat's Learning Library**, *see the back endpaper.*

The Cat in the Hat's Learning Library
The Cat in the
Learning Librar

The editors would like to thank
BARBARA KIEFER, Ph.D.,
Charlotte S. Huck Professor of Children's Literature,
The Ohio State University, and
LISA KATHLEEN GRADDY,
Deputy Chair and Curator, Division of Political History,
National Museum of American History, Smithsonian Institution,
for their assistance in the preparation of this book.

TM & copyright © by Dr. Seuss Enterprises, L.P. 2016
THE CAT IN THE HAT'S LEARNING LIBRARY logos and word mark are registered trademarks of
Dr. Seuss Enterprises, L.P.
THE CAT IN THE HAT'S LEARNING LIBRARY logos © Dr. Seuss Enterprises, L.P. 1998

THE CAT IN THE HAT KNOWS A LOT ABOUT THAT! logo and word mark TM 2010 Dr. Seuss
Enterprises, L.P., Portfolio Entertainment, Inc., and Collingwood O'Hare Productions, Ltd.
All rights reserved. The PBS KIDS logo is a registered trademark of PBS. Both are used with
permission. All rights reserved.

All rights reserved. Published in the United States by Random House Children's Books,
a division of Penguin Random House LLC, New York.

Random House and the colophon are registered trademarks of Penguin Random House LLC.

Visit us on the Web!
Seussville.com
randomhousekids.com

Educators and librarians, for a variety of teaching tools, visit us at RHTeachersLibrarians.com

Library of Congress Cataloging-in-Publication Data
Names: Worth, Bonnie, author. | Ruiz, Aristides, ill. | Mathieu, Joe, ill.
Title: One vote, two votes, I vote, you vote : all about voting / by Bonnie Worth ;
illustrated by Aristides Ruiz and Joe Mathieu.
Description: New York : Random House, 2016. | Series: The Cat in the Hat's learning library
Identifiers: LCCN 2015041949 | ISBN 978-0-399-55598-5 (trade) | ISBN 978-0-399-55599-2 (lib. bdg.)
ISBN 978-1-5247-1633-2 (pbk.)
Subjects: LCSH: Voting—United States—Juvenile literature. |
Elections—United States—Juvenile literature.
Classification: LCC JK1978 .W67 2016 | DDC 324.6/50973—dc23

Printed in the United States of America   10 9 8 7 6 5 4 3 2 1

Random House Children's Books supports the First Amendment and celebrates the right to read.

One Vote, Two Votes, I Vote, You Vote

by Bonnie Worth

illustrated by Aristides Ruiz and Joe Mathieu

The Cat in the Hat's Learning Library®

Random House 🏠 New York

Voting is something
we do every day.
It's a way we can choose
that gives us our own say.

class trip:
.museum

2. zoo

3. beach

class pet:
. gerbil

2. guinea pig

3. goldfish

.lass snack:
apple

2. carrot

3. grapes

CLASS ELECTIONS
✓ TODAY ☺

We vote for class president,
and which snack to get,
where to go on class trip,
what to pick as class pet.

7

Voting gives each of us
our very own voice.
It allows a large group
to make ONE single choice.

HOW DO YOU VOTE?

With a proudly raised hand,

marks on paper,

thumbs up or thumbs down—
understand?

Can you choose NOT to vote?
Yes, but that's a sure way
to lose your own voice
and to not have a say.

The item or person
that most of us select
will wind up the winner—
the one we elect.

Are presidents important?
Oh, yes, they are—very!
They head up the government
and the military.

Vice presidents take over
on the unhappy day
when presidents get sick
or else pass away.

Every four years,
we elect them, you see,
because we live in
a DEMOCRACY—
a government
FOR the people
and run BY them, too,
which means that
this country
is governed by YOU.

Every two years, we elect senators
and congresspeople of our choice
to make laws in Washington
and be our state's voice.

We also elect sheriffs
and mayors and such.
Do local elections count?
You bet, just as much!

MAYER
for
MAYOR

DRUDGE
FOR
JUDGE

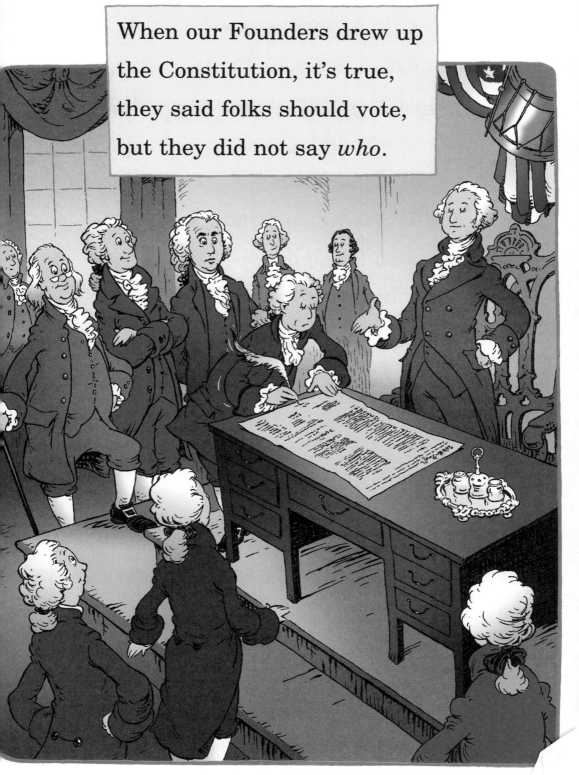

When our Founders drew up
the Constitution, it's true,
they said folks should vote,
but they did not say *who*.

Since then, our history
is marked by brave fights
waged by people who struggled
to win voting rights
for all of the races
and for all womankind,
and also for eighteen-
year-olds, bear in mind.

Voting Rights Timeline:

1870

1920

15TH Amendment:
BLACK MEN CAN VOTE.

19TH Amendment:
WOMEN CAN VOTE.

That means that quite soon
you will get to vote, too.
So please pay attention.
This matters to YOU!

1924

CITIZENSHIP ACT:
NATIVE AMERICANS
CAN VOTE.

1971

26TH Amendment:
18-YEAR-OLDS
CAN VOTE.

Only citizens can vote
and, as you've just been told,
people who are at least
eighteen years old.

TOWN HALL

VOTE

REGISTER

VOTER REGISTRATION

REGISTER
HERE TO
VOTE

You must sign up in person
or on the Internet
with name, address, and birth date.
And one more thing yet:

18

You can write down your party,

if you do not mind.

Cakes and ice cream, you're thinking?

Is the party that kind?

THIS kind of party,
I'm here to report,
is the kind that we know as
the political sort.

DEMOCRATIC PARTY

REPUBLICAN PARTY

It's made up of large
groups of citizens who
share beliefs and ideas
and opinions, too.

LIBERTARIAN PARTY

GREEN PARTY

INDEPENDENT

Democrats and Republicans
are the biggest two.
Plus small parties to pick from—
more than just a few.

DEMOCRATIC CANDIDATES:

 ✓ SNOW

 ☐ DOE

 ☐ FLOW

 ☐ ROW

REPUBLICAN CANDIDATES:

 ☐ FINNER

 ☐ RINNER

 ✗ SKINNER

 ☐ ZINNER

In primary elections
(run before November),
votes will be cast
by each party member
for the candidate who,
they hope and they pray,
will be on the ballot
come Election Day.

SNOW vs. SKINNER

Candidates set out
on the campaign trail
to convince voters
that they will not fail.

"A vote for me,"
the candidates say,
"will make your dreams
come true someday."

With speeches and ads
and town hall meetings,
with handshakes and waves
and cheery greetings,
they work to win
the voters' trust.
To win nomination,
this is a must.

I may be wrong,
but it does seem to me
that voting is one BIG
responsibility!

As a voter, you must
follow news carefully.
You should read, watch, and listen,
and then try to see
what the candidates,
if elected, plan to do.
What are their beliefs?
Do they ring true for you?

THING 2

FOCUS
ON
YOU!

Debates are held
for the people to see
the candidates talk
on live TV!

Moderators on hand
have questions to ask.
To give their best answer
is the candidates' task.

A debate is an argument
that's meant to sway.
It is run by rules
in a most formal way.

At meetings called rallies,
supporters get out
to cheer the candidate
they care most about.

VOTE T-1

MORE FUN WITH THING 1

VOTE T-1

VOTE T-1

WIN WITH 1

GET IT DONE with THING 1

Supporters on the phone
or going door-to-door say,
"Vote for my party
on Election Day!"

They raise lots of money,
collect change in jars,
and sell campaign stickers
to stick on cars!

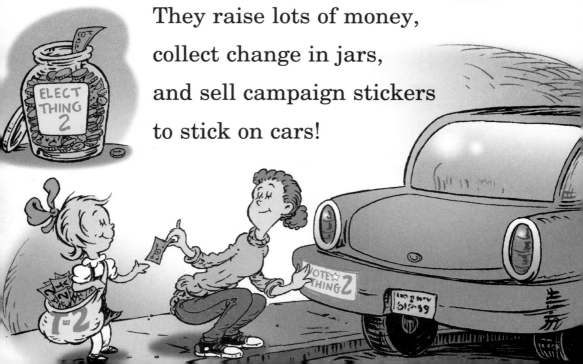

George Washington won the vote,
so I have been told,
during a winter
that was snowy and cold.

1788

In 1845,
Congress passed a vote to say
there would be an earlier
Election Day.

NOVEMBER

The day, each year,
is easy to remember.
It's the Tuesday after the first
Monday in November.

This date was chosen
for a very good reason.
It came at the end of
the harvesting season.

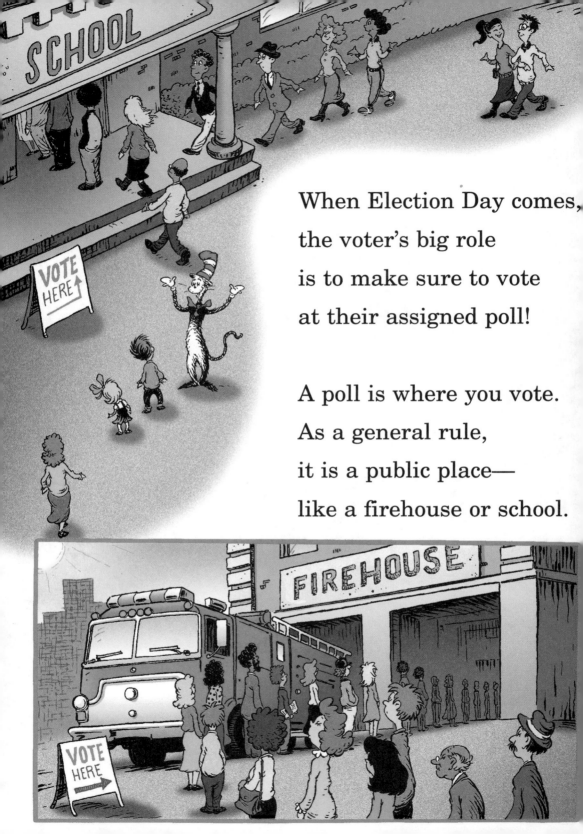

When Election Day comes,
the voter's big role
is to make sure to vote
at their assigned poll!

A poll is where you vote.
As a general rule,
it is a public place—
like a firehouse or school.

If you're out of town,

there's a chance that you might

mail an absentee ballot.

Voting is your right!

People cast their votes
by different means—
ballots fed into computers
or direct voting machines.

However you vote,
it's important, you see,
that voters are given
complete privacy!

A curtain or screen
protects voters from view.
This ensures that your vote
is known only to YOU.

The polls close up
at the end of the day.
Here come the counters!
Please clear the way!

By special computer,
poll results are scanned.
But some votes are still
counted out by hand.

The results are sent
to the Board of Elections,
which declares the winner
after careful inspections.

The loser admits their bitter defeat.

The winner announces
their victory sweet!

The winner vows to serve
everyone in the land—
not just the supporters
who lent them a hand.

Woo-hoo
for
THING 2!

If all of this rings true,
it is my dearest hope that . . .

you will cast your first vote
for the Cat in the Hat!

GLOSSARY

Absentee: A person who is expected to be somewhere but is not.

Ballot: The act of or process of voting, usually on paper, and in secret.

Campaign: A series of acts intended to achieve a particular goal.

Candidate: A person who applies for a job or is nominated for election.

Citizen: A legally recognized member of a state or country.

Electronic: Referring to a device having computer parts.

Inspection: A close study.

Moderator: A person who directs a debate or discussion.

Nominate: To propose someone to run for office.

Political: Having to do with government affairs.

Poll: The place where voting takes place or the act of voting.

Responsibility: The state of having a duty.

Scan: To read, with the eye or by electronic means.

Sway: To convince or change someone's mind by means of speech or argument.

FOR FURTHER READING

I Could Do That!: Esther Morris Gets Women the Vote by Linda Arms White, illustrated by Nancy Carpenter (Farrar, Straus and Giroux, Melanie Kroupa Books). The story of a spirited young woman who won the vote for women in the Wyoming Territory in 1869. A Bank Street Best Children's Book of the Year. For kindergarten and up.

If I Were President by Catherine Stier, illustrated by DyAnne DiSalvo-Ryan (Albert Whitman & Company). Six children take turns posing as president of the United States in this simple look at the various responsibilities of the president. For kindergarten and up.

Lillian's Right to Vote: A Celebration of the Voting Rights Act of 1965 by Jonah Winter, illustrated by Shane W. Evans (Random House, Schwartz & Wade). As a hundred-year-old African American woman walks up the hill to her polling place, she looks back on her family's history and the history of the fight for voting rights. An author's note includes information about the real woman who inspired Lillian. For kindergarten and up.

Vote! by Eileen Christelow (Clarion Books). This award-winning book about a mayoral election—told in comic-book style—is an accessible and fun introduction to all the steps involved in an election. For grades 1 and up.

INDEX